learn to play
keyboard

GW00672302

Published by **Wise Publications**

Exclusive Distributors: Music Sales Limited,
14-15 Berners Street, London W1T 3LJ, UK

Order No. AM1009162
ISBN 978-1-78305-624-8

Edited by Ruth Power.
Inside layout by Fresh Lemon.

Made in China.

www.musicsales.com

Introduction

This playbook will get you playing the keyboard in no time!

You'll learn the basic techniques you need, some essential chords and how to read music.

Let's get started!

Contents

Playing position

A good playing position means that you'll be comfortable at the keyboard, and, more importantly, you'll be more likely to play well.

Sit facing the middle of the keyboard with your feet opposite the pedals and try to keep a reasonably straight back.

Avoid tension in any part of your body, particularly in your lower arms.

Make sure you don't slump over the keyboard.

Tip:

An adjustable piano stool is better than an ordinary chair, because it allows people of differing statures to play in comfort.

Make sure your seat is at a height which allows your lower arms to sit level with, or just above, the keys.

Fingering

Fingering is a system designed to prevent your fingers getting tangled up in knots. It works like this:

Each finger is given a number, as shown in the photograph below. You will see these numbers over the notes in the music – they tell you which fingers to use for those notes.

Try to stick to the recommended fingerings for each piece and you will soon assume the habit of having your hands in the correct position.

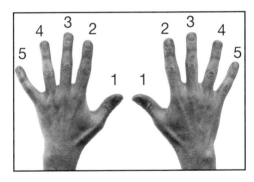

5 4 3 2 1 1 2 3 4 5

11

Hand positions

Your hands should be supported from the wrist – it's very important that you don't permit your wrists to descend below the keyboard.

Now, with your fingers sitting lightly above the keys, curl your fingers slightly as if gently holding an imaginary ball. Your fingertips should cover five adjacent notes in each hand.

This is the normal five finger position, to which your hand will eventually return automatically.

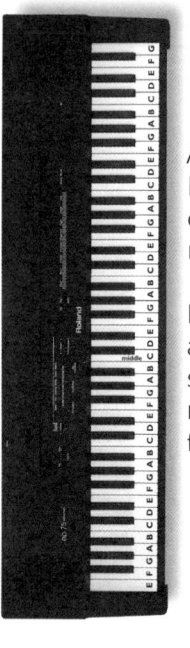

At first glance, the keyboard may seem confusing – so many notes!

But the keyboard is actually just the same series of 12 notes repeated over and over, for its entire length!

This is the section that we deal with in this playbook:

Only seven letter names are used.

The black keys are arranged in twos and threes in a repeating pattern – this irregularity is actually very useful, because it enables you to find your way around the keyboard.

Reading music

It's best if you learn how to read music as part of learning to play keyboard. Reading music is easy – once you understand the fundamentals you'll take to it in no time.

There are two basic elements to the way music is written: pitch and duration.

Pitch tells you how high or low a note is (low is to the left on the keyboard, high is to the right), and duration tells you how long the note is played for, and when it is played in relation to other notes around it.

The five lines on which the notes are placed are called a **stave**.

A note placed on top of the stave is higher than a note placed at the bottom.

For keyboard players there is a stave for the left hand and one for the right. In the early part of this playbook we will concern ourselves with the right hand only.

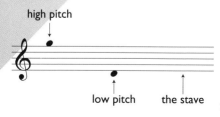

high pitch

low pitch   the stave

Rhythm

If you look at any piece of music you can see that notes have different shapes – some have tails, some have solid note heads, while others are hollow.

They will soon become very familiar to you.

This symbol is called a **whole note**, or semibreve, and lasts for the duration of a full bar, so it has a count of four beats.

Against the count of 1 – 2 – 3 – 4 you would count whole notes like this:

| 1 | 2 | 3 | 4 |

𝐨

This symbol is called a **half note**, or minim, and lasts for two beats.

Against the count of 1 – 2 – 3 – 4 you would count half notes like this:

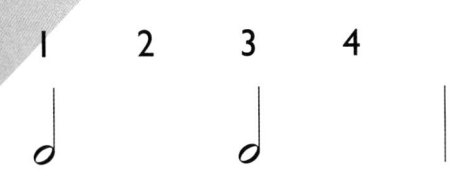

Finally, this symbol is called a **quarter note**, or crotchet, and lasts for one beat. Thus there are four of these to every bar.

Against the count of 1 – 2 – 3 – 4 you would count quarter notes like this:

Bars

Music has a basic pulse or beat; multiples of these beats are grouped into larger units called **bars** or measures.

Bars are made up of groups of beats – when you tap your foot to a piece of music, you're responding to the beat.

How many beats there are within each bar is indicated by a symbol called a **time signature**.

Time signatures

The most common grouping of beats is 4 in a bar: this is sometimes called **common time**, and we'll be using this initially.

𝐂 = common time

Try counting steadily from 1 to 4 and then repeating that sequence:

1 – 2 – 3 – 4 / 1 – 2 – 3 – 4 / etc

Each time you count '1' you are beginning a new bar.

 Common time is also sometimes written like this, with 4 quarter notes to a bar.

23

Your first notes

The easiest way to locate a white key is to see where it fits into the pattern of black keys.

Look for the groups of two black keys, and then find the white key in the middle of these. This note is D. C is directly to the left of D – or to the left of the group of two black keys.

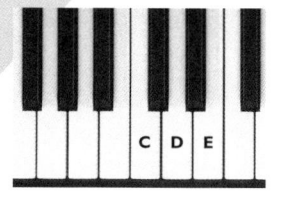

The groups of black keys are repeated all the way up the keyboard so there are lots of Cs. In order to distinguish between them we usually refer to one of them as middle C, which is the one closest to, or in the centre of the keyboard.

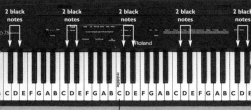

This is how middle C looks on the stave:

Notice that middle C occupies a small line directly under the main stave. This is called a **leger line**.

Leger lines enable us to write notes which are higher or lower than the stave's five lines and four spaces.

Here is the note **D** which you first found in between the groups of 2 black notes.

Make sure you play the one directly to the right of middle C.

On one side of the
note D you found C
– on the other side is
the note **E**.

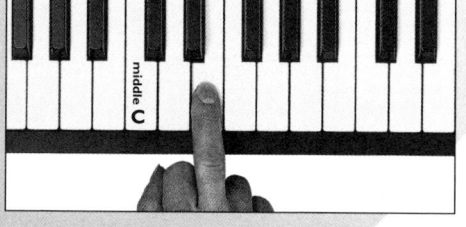

Playing C, D & E

Next is a tune to help you learn where these notes are. Play C with the thumb on your right hand, and D and E with your index and middle fingers respectively.

The fingering numbers should help you to remember which fingers to use.

Watch out for the one bar rest after each group of three notes. The count written over the music should help you with the rhythm, while the names of the notes are written underneath the stave.

Count: 1 2 3 4 1 2 3 4 1 2 3 4 1 2 3 4

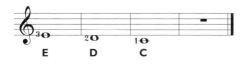

Right-hand notes

F

middle C

middle C

The notes F, G, A & B

Look at your keyboard and notice the repeating pattern of three black keys – you can use these to find the white keys around and between them.

Reading from the left, they are F, G, A and B. Practise finding each note and say the letter name out loud as you play the note.

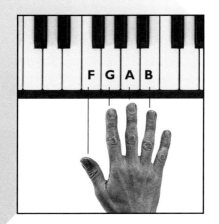

TIP

If you're having trouble memorising the names and locations of all the notes, try placing labelled stickers onto the keys.

Playing F, G, A & B

Now that you are familiar with counting beats and bars, let's try an exercise that familiarises you with these four new notes, while also teaching you to count in units of two beats each.

For this exercise play the lower note F with the thumb of your right hand, keeping the relaxed hand position you learned earlier.

The notes in this exercise change after two beats, so you have to think a little quicker than in the previous exercise.

Keep your other fingers 'hovering'
over the other notes.

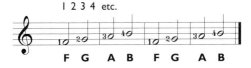

Clefs

The symbol at the beginning of music tells us which hand to play.

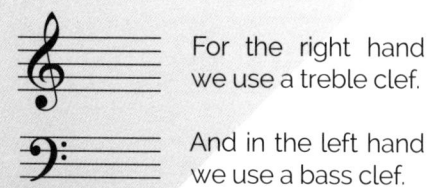

For the right hand we use a treble clef.

And in the left hand we use a bass clef.

Middle C is shown on each clef here:

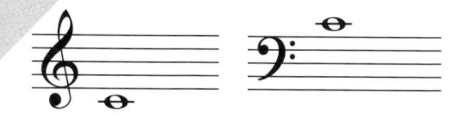

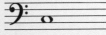

middle C

D Left-hand notes

middle C

F Left-hand notes

middle C

Left-hand summary

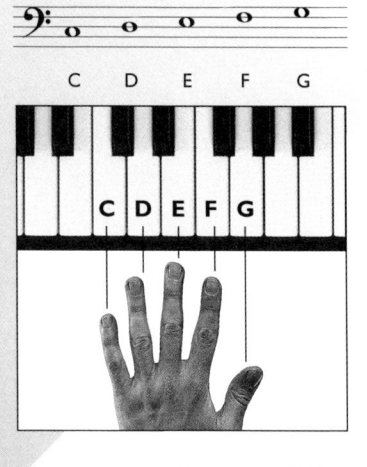

From now on we will show all the notes on both staves, with treble and bass clefs.

Rests

Now we will look at what the music tells us when you are not playing. The symbols occupying the spaces where you are not playing are called rests, and they have similar rhythmic values to notes. This is how they work:

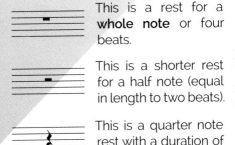

This is a rest for a **whole note** or four beats.

This is a shorter rest for a half note (equal in length to two beats).

This is a quarter note rest with a duration of one beat.

You can combine these rests. For example, to have a part silent for three beats you would combine the two beat half note rest with the one beat quarter note rest giving a total of three beats rest.

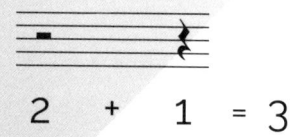

2 + 1 = 3

You can also combine notes using a **tie**. A tie adds the value of one note to another.

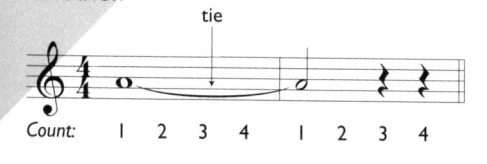

Here's an exercise designed to get you used to playing with the left hand. Look out for the different rests throughout.

Well done!

You now know seven notes in the right hand, and five notes in the left hand.

To sum up, play through each note slowly, reminding yourself of the note name and its relation to the stave and the keyboard.

Right-hand notes:

Left-hand notes:

Chords

A chord is created when you play more than one note simultaneously. You can do this with the right or left hand, or with both at once. There are many different types of chord, but here are a few simple shapes you can master in minutes.

Right-hand chords
Most notes in a chord are played in the right hand, so that's a good place to start. Later we will add more notes to our chords by introducing the left hand.

Chords with both hands

Now let's add the left hand. Generally, when playing chords, the left hand plays fewer notes than the right, and they are more widely spaced.

The left and right hands don't play separate chords; they simply share the job of playing the notes of one chord.

These chords are shown in notation and a photograph as before, and also in a handy chord diagram highlighting which keys to play.

Both hands together

Practise the following exercise one hand at a time before playing with both hands together.

Once again, hand and finger positions are crucial – you should be able to play this exercise without dramatically moving your hand up and down the keys.

From the one basic hand position you have been using so far you should be able to play all the notes in this piece.

TIP:
If you have a tempo control on your keyboard, use it to learn the pieces at a slower speed; then you can gradually come up to the proper speed.

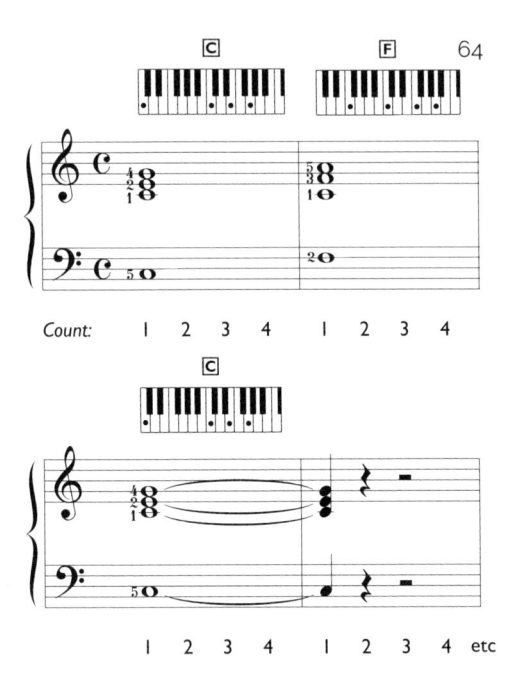

Count: 1 2 3 4 | 1 2 3 4

1 2 3 4 | 1 2 3 4 etc

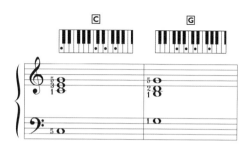

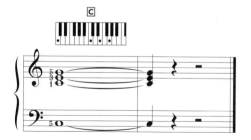

More tempos

Another common grouping of beats is 3 in a bar. This is sometimes referred to as 'waltz' time.

Count steadily to 3 and keep repeating. Try to feel the emphasis on the first beat of the bar and the rhythm of the tempo.

1 – 2 – 3 / 1 – 2 – 3 / 1 – 2 – 3 / etc

This symbol is called a dotted half note and lasts for 3 beats. The dot after the half note has the effect of adding half the half note's length to it: you hold the note for 3 beats.

1 – 2 – 3

A new note

Now it's time to look at one more note-value: the **eighth-note**, or quaver.

Eighth notes are the shortest notes that you're going to play in this playbook. They last for half a beat and require accurate counting.

On their own eighth notes are written with a curved flag attached to the stem, but are bracketed together with a beam when groups occur, to make them easier to read.

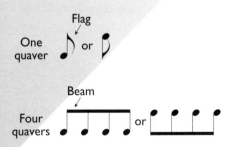

69

Counting eighth notes

Eighth notes split the quarter note beat in half; in a $\frac{4}{4}$ bar they are counted like this:

Count: 1 & 2 & 3 & 4 &

beam   beam

An easy way of remembering the duration of combined eighth notes and quarter notes is (without playing) to call a quarter note 'tea' and two eighth notes 'coffee'.

Look at the example below and say the words under the stave rhythmically.

tea   cof - fee tea   tea

tea   cof - fee tea   (break)

Your first song

You're now ready to try playing a complete song: Jingle Bells!

Remember to follow the music carefully, and you won't have any problems with this simple melody.

Keep the left hand steady throughout and concentrate on getting the melody right.

Jingle Bells

What you've learnt

In a very short space of time you've covered a lot of ground and you're already well on your way to being able to learn and play many more great songs for keyboard.

You've learnt:
- correct posture at the keyboard
- where to place your fingers on the keys
- how to play with both hands together
- how to read music notation
- how to count note lengths
- playing in time.

Suggested listening

We've suggested some songs you might like to try to learn, and also some books to further your knowledge and skills. Keep up the good work!

'**Let it Be**' (The Beatles)

'**Candle In The Wind**' (Elton John)

'**What'd I Say**' (Ray Charles)

'**Fallin'**' (Alicia Keys)

'**Love Song**' (Sara Bareilles)

'**Bohemian Rhapsody**' (Queen)

'**Imagine**' (John Lennon)

'**Chariots of Fire**' (Vangelis)

'**Light My Fire**' (The Doors)

'**Piano Man**' (Billy Joel)

'**Superstition**' (Stevie Wonder)

'**The Scientist**' (Coldplay)

'**Lucille**' (Little Richard)

'**Your Song**' (Elton John)

'**Someone Like You**' (Adele)

'**Angel**' (Sarah McLachlan)

More learning

Playbook Keyboard Chords
AM1008403

**The Complete Keyboard Player
Book 1 (Tutor Book)** AM91383

FastForward: Cool Blues Keyboard
AM934835

**FastForward: Dynamic Rock
Keyboards** AM92437

MORE IN THE Playbook SERIES

available from all good music shops
or, in case of difficulty contact: music@musicsales.co.uk